Make Me Your Love Song

Make Me Your Love Song

Poems by

Peggy Schimmelman

© 2024 Peggy Schimmelman. All rights reserved.
This material may not be reproduced in any form, published,
reprinted, recorded, performed, broadcast,
rewritten, or redistributed without
the explicit permission of Peggy Schimmelman.
All such actions are strictly prohibited by law.

Cover design by Shay Culligan
Cover art by Crawford Jolly on Unsplash
Author photo by Paul Schimmelman

ISBN: 978-1-63980-612-6

Kelsay Books
502 South 1040 East, A-119
American Fork, Utah 84003
Kelsaybooks.com

Acknowledgments

Thank you to the following publications, in which versions of these poems previously appeared:

Double Take: "Music Man," "Familiar Shores"
Eunoia: "Porch Step Twelve Bar Blues"
Haight Ashbury Literary Journal: "Carnival Days," "Oops, You Missed It!"
Mused—Bella Online: "Missouri Midnight"
Naugatuck Review: "In the Safeway Checkout Line"
Peregrine Journal: "Mis Information"
Pyrokinection: "Cozumel Moon"
Rock, Paper, Poem: "The Odds"
Synkronociti: "An Empty Tip Jar"
Wild Musette: "A Poem in Three"

Included in the poetry chapbook *Crazytown* (Writing Knights Press): "Parting Shot," "The Last Lullaby," "That Song in Your Head"

Included in the poetry chapbook *Tick Tock* (Finishing Line Press): "Nocturne," "Rebellion," "Tick Tock"

Contents

A Poem in Three	13
Music Man	14
This Song Is for You, He Said	16
On Love and Politics	17
Love Bites	18
The Odds	20
The Timekeeper	
(Friday in the VA Hospital Dining Hall)	22
The Last Lullaby	23
On My Walk to the Farmers' Market	24
Through My Living Room Window	26
Nocturne	27
The Hunter's Moon (A Perspective)	28
The Button Tin (1958)	30
At Your Bedside, Waiting	32
In the Safeway Check-Out Line	34
Missouri Midnight	36
Porch Step Twelve-Bar Blues	37
El Duende	
(Spirit of Flamenco)	38
That Song in Your Head	40
On the 425th Night of the Virus	42
Parting Shot	44
Cozumel Moon	45
No Fan of Heavy Metal (for Marguerite)	46
Tick-Tock	48
Push Through This Night	49
Rebellion	50
Music to My Ears	51
Marching Music	52
An Empty Tip Jar	54
Carnival Days	56

Mis Information	57
Familiar Shores	58
Oops, You Missed It	60
Seventy-Eight Degrees and Sunny	62
Look Up!	64

A Poem in Three

Make me your love song
in three-quarter time
conjure me, count me in
one-two-three-*one*-two-three
whisper me whistle me
dance me romance me
woo me infuse me
with rhythm and rhyme.

I'm a Viennese ballroom
a Tennessee dive
I'm denim and crinoline
sawdust and silver
seduce me unloose me
unwrap me undo me
inhale me consume me
I'm whiskey I'm wine.

I'll Waltz Across Texas
I'm Norwegian Wood
I'm Strauss and Chopin
Jolie Blon, Clementine
so wrangle untangle me
Mr. Bojangle me
I'm Amazing Grace
Sweet Betsy from Pike.

I'm Scarborough Fair
on a Moon River night
so Piano Man stun me
come fiddle-strum-drum me
croon me retune me
twirl and unfurl me
then swing me and sing me
in three-quarter time.

Music Man

I like my men
like I like my music
bold
with a confident rhythm
strong
on the downbeat
snappy
on the backbeat
unafraid of a little
im
p
r o
visation
or   syncopation
and lively
as a Cajun fiddle.

Some like a man
who's tuned to perfection
steady
as a symphony
soft
as a love song
smooth
as a tango
and classy
as a vintage Amati.

I can dig all that
but I like me a man
who can swing me
rock me
and set my foot tapping—
make me dance in the street
like New Orleans jazz.

This Song Is for You, He Said

Your memory circles my bed
armed and threatening
its weapons a resonant voice and acoustic guitar
a serenade featuring that love song you wrote:
the sweet tune I ridiculed before I knew
how mockery could slice and scar.

I wonder if you ever wrote another.
It's years too late for apologies
but I wish you could know my remorse
for that careless giggle
the dismissive shrug

my spontaneous response
which might have been different
had I understood then as I do now
how scorn can poison a creative spirit

had I realized that every tune
like every poem, is somebody's
baby, a labor of love
and had I known yours was to be
the only song a lover
would ever write about me.

Had I known that years later
though I can't recall the shape of your eyes
or the sound of your laugh
sometimes at night I still hear your song,
its every word etched on my memory.

On Love and Politics

Words you want to believe
fall so easy on your ears
you could stand for hours
mesmerized
under a soothing
shower of confirmation
your doubts scrubbed away
along with a balanced perspective:

down the drain they swirl
so far from your sight
you'll forget
that you ever embraced them.

Love Bites

A pinch, a sting
and off you go:
bitten, smitten
prancing in the sun—
it's that kind of day:

a lasso the wind kind of day
a straddle the breeze
head thrown back
one hand on the reins
the other waving wild
a giggly, giddy
ride 'em cowgirl
wahoo!
kind of day, until . . .

the wind beneath you dies
and now you're falling
down, down
and here you lie
on that bed you made for yourself
and you wonder again
if maybe this time
you should not have flown
quite so high

and yet you suspect that
given the chance
you'll rope that wind
and ride it again
and you'll ride it the same

because such is the folly
of the human condition:
once love-bug bitten
our hearts don't remember
any other way to ride.

The Odds

Scientists say the odds of either of us
existing right now are slightly less
than one in 400 quadrillion
taking into account
the chances of our ancestors meeting
feeling attracted, procreating
and the subsequent chain of copulation
a series of merging egg and sperm
that resulted in the eventual, specific
but random combination of nucleotides
that created the unique specimen
that is you or I.

Yet here we are: against the odds
yokefellows plowing life's field together
raising babies, burying fathers
and at this moment
consuming our burgers on the Ale House patio
taking for granted each other's company
and that of Todd, our affable waiter
who had a one in 400 quadrillion chance
of serving us lunch today

all of us pondering what's up
with that middle-aged lady
in the cheery sundress and heart-shaped shades
who dances along the downtown streets
boom-box blaring on her shoulder
as she belts out lyrics along with Shakira
Sheryl Crow, Madonna—all of whom had
a one in 400 quadrillion chance
of being born at all, much less
of winning the pop star lottery.

What's her story? we wonder
as she boogies past us, beaming
singing, tossing us a wave
as if she knows how lucky we are
to be alive on this earth, in this country, this city,
on this street at this exact moment in time.
Her swaying hips ask: Why not smile?
Why not dance?
Why aren't you singing?
You have beaten the odds, after all.

The Timekeeper
(Friday in the VA Hospital Dining Hall)

His eyes catch mine and won't let go
as he propels his wheelchair toward me.
I read his lips: "Dance."
In the middle of "Oh Susannah"
I abandon my cajón.
While our volunteer band plays on
I grasp the wheelchair's arms.
Push and pull.
Dancing.
I sing along
but Kevin left his voice in Vietnam.

Again he mouths "dance," but I protest:
the band needs me.
Next up is "Buffalo Gals" and I blow it,
distracted by images of a younger Kevin
dancing by the light of the moon.
With his girlfriend, his daughter, his mother.
My time is all over the place.

The Last Lullaby

Selam and Adonay, hush now and sleep.
Boat man don't like it when little ones weep.
Ahead, Europe waits to shelter and feed us—
to welcome us. Children, now listen to me:

nightmares can't reach you out here on the sea.
Aziz and Rahwa, please hush now and sleep.
Visions of villages, ravaged and charred
will fade like ghosts, left to die on the water.

Eritrea, Gambia, Nigeria, Ghana
the souls of your slaughtered are singing to me.
Semirah and Hanna, hush now and sleep.
All boats list and lurch, there is nothing to fear:

with God watching over, rescue is near.
As we slip from the edge, slide into the deep,
Semirah, Hanna, Rahwa, Aziz,
Selam and Adonay, hush now and sleep.

On My Walk to the Farmers' Market

I set out at a jaunty pace
somewhere between a stroll and a power walk
greeting neighbors and yapping dogs
soaking up September sunshine
at one with the world
my spirit at peace.

But then I turn a corner
and recent tragedies invade my thoughts:
Israel and Gaza
floods and earthquakes
more than ten thousand victims
and countless devastated survivors.

Another left turn
and matters close to home start to prickle:
my son's new job
my friend's diagnosis
and my own possibly shrinking
well of creativity.

At the busy 4th Street intersection
again my anxiety swerves
as the worries settle into my hips
slow my stride and threaten to turn
a ten-minute walk into twenty.

I shift my anxieties into reverse
refocus on the misery of those left behind
when their homes and families were taken.
I wonder how they can bear it:
their grief and guilt so intense
their pain so much greater than mine.

Then as I rest on a bench, peace returns
as all around me familiar faces
each with their own set of worries
peruse produce, local honey and wine
exploring Mother Earth's bounty
while on the rotunda Jack Quigley plays on—

all of us soothing our private anxieties
in a communal celebration of life.

Through My Living Room Window

I glanced up from my puzzle and saw them:
a young couple herding two kids down the sidewalk
on their way to the rodeo parade.

There was something about
the woman's straw sunhat
the daughter's bright chatter
as she skipped along
in those pink, fringed cowgirl boots,
the father's urging
as the toddler dawdled
one tiny hand clasping
some treasure he'd found.
"C'mon buddy," said his papa.
"Let's go see the horses,"
and he hoisted the child to his shoulders.

A twenty-second scene.
An ache in my throat.
Ambushed again:
I never see you coming
with your sword dipped in honey.
Ah, sweet nostalgia,
why must you cut so deep?

Nocturne

Something not quite right
in that restless
wide awake night
stars slipping out
of cozy constellations
like teenage daughters
through bedroom windows
embracing boyfriends
beneath a leering
lop-sided moon
while the humid breeze scolds
and the mockingbirds fret
like despairing mothers
whose fragile nests
have shifted off-kilter
tipped
and started
        to tumble
                through
                      time.

The Hunter's Moon (A Perspective)

She is full of herself tonight.
Brilliance blurs her edges,
spills over her borders, crashes
through your kitchen window
where you sit with a glass of reminiscence.

Mind if I join you?
She stalks your secrets, pounces
on the juiciest, most delectable one,
lures it, naked, into the open
where it cringes, bolts, slides, slithers
seeking escape. But she is relentless.

Then she whispers:
I was there, remember?
Yes, I was complicit.
But if you consider
the simultaneous horrors—
the tragedies I witnessed
each instant of that eventful night—
well, you might understand
how abetting your indiscretion
was for me a welcome distraction.

And though I read malintent
in his luminous eyes
I knew you'd survive, and besides
your naïve heart was ripe
for some schooling.
Anyway, I only contributed
a sprinkle of magic, the lunar cachet.

I mean, let's face it:
although not rightfully yours,
even without my influence
the man was darn near irresistible.

The Button Tin (1958)

To us it seemed ancient: a round dime-store box
faded and scratched, its lid a once colorful depiction
of Tom and Huck with fishing poles
short pants and straw hats
a lazy summer day at the river.

On rainy days you would sit us down
a circle of sisters on the cracked linoleum
with needle and thread, words of instruction
and this boxful of buttons
salvaged from decades of garments
relegated through the years to the ragbag.

Some were as plain as our hand-me-down blouses
others sturdy as a wool coat of grandpa's
or drab olive green like dad's work clothes
and a handful of tiny reminders
of the layette you sewed for our brother
when store-bought wasn't an option.

But my favorites were a set of seven
exotic and bold, a vibrant scarlet
adorned with a splash of gold sparkles.
I liked to imagine you had traveled one time
to the orient and brought home a dress
that you wore when my dad took you dancing.

I pictured you twirling in a red silk sheath
sleek and shiny with fancy buttons
enchanting my father
(who must have been handsome and happy then,
mesmerized by your merry dark eyes)

in the years before your days became filled
with afternoon soaps and housekeeping drudgery
supper to cook, a succession of offspring
distorting your once slim figure

before you ever conceived of four small girls
cross-legged, giggling on the bedroom floor
weaving necklaces, bracelets
from threads of your past
adding here a diamond, there a pearl
plucked from a child's imagination.

At Your Bedside, Waiting

A minute can feel like an hour.
I touch your cheek, stroke your hand
survey the monitors.
I try to believe.

On average
1.8 humans perish each second.
More than 100 billion souls
have passed through this world.
How many haloes does Heaven have left?
How much room in the fiery furnace
where an hour must feel like eons?

A memory can slice through decades,
soothe like a sunbeam
sting like a scorpion.
Or both:

You were seven, I was nine.
Stick-horse cowgirls
sucking on cherry Tootsie Roll pops,
building a fort from fallen tree limbs
romping in the woods behind our house.
Busy Bee, they called you then
A bright-eyed cotton-top
inventing, exploring, never bored.
Never still.
Endless summer vacation.
Twelve weeks can feel like a year.

I brush back your hair
whisper "I'm here."
In the rush of an angel's wings
another two souls have moved on.

Death whistles a dirge up the stairwell.
Across the corridor, a man of God prays.
I touch your cheek
stroke your motionless hand
survey the monitors.
I try to believe.

An afternoon can feel like a lifetime.

In the Safeway Check-Out Line

The woman ahead of us
plunked items onto the counter
as if she regretted her choices
and wished to return
the whole mundane lot
to the shelves.
My son, a cherubic three-year-old
clutching a donut in one hand
a Pterodactyl in the other
peered up at her, curious
then beamed as he turned to me
with what to him seemed
an astute observation:
"She's ugly."

I choked on chagrin
 my response a hurried
"No, she isn't," to him
 a guilty glance at her
as she muttered "Nice manners"
and looked away—hard to tell
if that arrow was aimed
at the angel-faced demon-child
who had wrecked her day
or at the incompetent mother
who had spawned him.

I followed her wounded eyes
along with those of the appalled cashier
to the glaring white clock on the wall—
and in that moment we formed
a triangular circuit
our singular thought revealed
in a harmonious trio of sighs:

Oh dear God
it's not even noon yet,
as the imp crammed the donut
into his pocket
rubbed powdered sugar into his hair
and declared that he needed to pee.

Missouri Midnight

Branches of sycamores
demonic silhouettes
dancing on a midnight wind
scrape against my windowpane
like an unsettled spirit
begging entry.

To the ominous chant
of the whippoorwills
lamenting, beseeching,
a restless apparition
wanders my halls
floorboards creaking
from the weight
of a guilty lover's
imagination.

A pale moon casts
a ghostly spotlight
across my half-empty bed
conjuring demons
inviting ghosts
of memories better left
undisturbed.

Porch Step Twelve-Bar Blues

Some nights the blues just keep on comin'
and all you can do is strum that guitar
hummin' some twelve-bar three chord tune
about a moonstruck mama
or a gamblin' man
or your damn empty wallet
and you wail it to the stars 'cause so far
nobody else seems to want to listen.

So you throw in a verse about God's indifference
not paying attention, not fixing the holes
in your low-down, bottomed-out, not-fair luck.
You're not asking much:
a little cash above rent money
lovin' in the midnight
a low-light, open mic blues jam
where people let you play your music.

Now thunder's rollin' in like a drunked-up drummer
heavy on the downbeat
draggin' on the backbeat
jackin' up the time
messin' with your shuffle.

But you can't quit now
got to write 'em where you find 'em
rope 'em in before they run

'cause your muse is in the porch swing
with one eye on the highway.
Why, tomorrow that girl might hit the road thumbin'
but tonight those blues just keep on comin'.

El Duende
(Spirit of Flamenco)

He senses the spirit
and opens his soul.
Bassist and bass—
tocador and guitarra
melt into one.

Bewitched fingers
on enchanted strings
weave tendrils of magic.
Possessed bailadores
are lifted and twirled.
Bedazzled they stamp
their emphatic percussion.
Castanets click while
enraptured cantantes
wail tales of lost love
sorrowful, familiar
and timeless.

Bailadores twirl
cantantes wail
castanets click
fingers snap
while boots tap rhythm
tocadores and guitarras
spinning their magic.

You and I watching
are swept up
transported
along with bailadores
cantantes, tocadores

through the ancient
star-drenched
Andalusian night
we sail, mesmerized
captives in the arms
of el duende.

That Song in Your Head

That random, mind-tickling snippet of melody
stops by uninvited—a mere distraction at first
but like a visiting in-law, outstaying its welcome—
persistent, intrusive
urging a song to your lips
whether you want it or not
as if you've nothing more important to do
than to walk around humming all day
a line or two of this long-ago tune
the title of which eludes you.

But without it, wouldn't your head be spinning
with your boss's demands
or that bill from your dentist
your mother's prognosis
your brother's addiction
or the stories you read in the morning news?
Distressing yes, but beyond your control.
And that fight with your husband
at breakfast this morning—
does it help to rewind and replay and relive it
revising the script as the day wears on?

So I say:
Welcome, earworm.
Walk right in and rock my soul
with your doo-wah-ditty memory:

a high-school dance,
socks on the gym floor,
nothing more to worry about
than my hair going frizzy
in the humid Ozark night
and whether or not
Donnie Joe Parker thinks
I'm the world's worst possible dancer.

On the 425th Night of the Virus

I awoke too soon
plagued by anxiety
too early to rise
but too late to hope
for any meaningful
additional sleep.

In this dark hour, I'm drawn
to your tranquil, rhythmic breathing
and to soothe my unease
I nestle close to the curve of your spine
tuck the blanket around us
and slip through the back door
of your dream.

Ah, there you are:
on stage with the band
caressing your bass,
September evening
at the Double Barrel wine bar,
Night Harvest live
on the jam-packed patio
where gypsy jazz flows
to enchant and excite
and drive to dance
the delighted, maskless
crowd.

From a table in back
I study your smile
how your eyes are lit
not from the flare of propane lamps
but from the power, the pride

the unabashed joy
that comes from making the music.

I didn't see it then, but now
as we huddle, unmoving and silent
locked inside this tuneless, viral darkness,
I see it, my love.
I see it.

Parting Shot

Through rivulets
on the shower door
I see
that lipstick red
goodbye
you scrawled
on the bathroom mirror—
taunting
cold
so final that
six months later
though I've scrubbed
and scrubbed
I can still
so clearly
read it.

Cozumel Moon

Inside your head, I imagine by now
there must be a billion old memories swarming
clamoring for your attention as midnight sails past
and you lie sleepless, a captive viewer
of that persistent, disconnected display.

Is one of those memories, I wonder, a girl
green-eyed and wild, just this side of crazy
Corona-tipsy and starlight-stoned
who traced inside a heart your name plus hers
in the sand where she taught you to samba
and to whisper *te amo,* bewitched as you were
by the light of the Cozumel moon?

The girl who once would've traded her soul
to be more than a memory hitching a ride
on an aging, randomly firing neuron
as midnight sails past and you lie sleepless
so far from the Cozumel moon.

No Fan of Heavy Metal (for Marguerite)

Friend, when you died so close to Christmas
the tree came down while the bells and carols
were replaced by a guilt-powered earworm:
Too late, it's too late.
So sorry. Forgive me.
Round and around. Repeat.

A few weeks prior, over coffee at Peet's
we'd talked of addictions, anxiety, hormones
that hour-long commute in rush-hour traffic.
Foolish me, pointing out your happy marriage
work you loved, your children's successes
as if sucking it up and counting our blessings
were a one size fits all solution.

If I'd only said this, suggested that
asked different questions, probed, insisted.
Instead, to lighten your mood
I asked if you'd heard about the guy back East
who chugged his beer, then flung the bottle
at a bartender's face for switching the tunes
from metal to Frosty the Snowman.

I might do the same, you told me.
if he had dissed Neil Young.
But not for Black Sabbath. No way.
And that was the last of a thousand times
your laugh lit my day, Marguerite.

If only I'd found the right words.
Even now, I'm stuck on the damning refrain:
Too late, it's too late.

So sorry. Forgive me.
Round and around. Repeat.

Turn that off, you would say.
It wasn't your fault. I forgive you.
But the song plays on as I fight the urge
to chug my beer and hurl the bottle
at that judgmental, invisible deejay
who won't change the tunes,
insisting I listen
to music I don't want to hear.

Tick-Tock

even now
while the meteors fly
on this Leonid night
and the lusty cat yowls
outside your transom

even now
with hope in remission
dreams in the closet
your gypsy soul
dances wild in the night

even now
as her jangling tambourine
demands contrition
for journeys not taken
inspiration wasted

even now
while your past is present
in fragmented swatches
know that your future
is revealing itself
one
tick tock
at a time.

Push Through This Night

Close your mind to the hordes
of nocturnal searchlights
probing the walls
of your agitated psyche
magnifying, amplifying
guilt, loss, and fear.

Push through this night
with its cruel jibes
and snide accusations.
Don't lend it your ear.
Soon dawn will arrive
in a river of light.
Float into the morning.
Push through this night.

Rebellion

My hips have gone pirate
provoking unrest
among thighs, discs, spine
their anarchic agenda forcing upon me
the unacceptable acceptance of aging—
that inevitable limp off the plank.
Their selfish revolt has foiled my efforts
to unify, strengthen mind, heart and lungs—
those more loyal factions who understand:

when Neptune beckons
and the ship's going down
there's all the more reason
to dance.

Music to My Ears

Tonight, I lie listening to the rain
the rain
the rain
such a sweet serenade
returning with a vengeance
determined, persistent
drenching the thirsty, drought-plagued earth
drowning my anxiety
my nocturnal fears flushed away by the rain
the rain
the rain.

Tonight, I'll forego my nightly prayers.
Anyway, God must tire
of my repetitive requests for blessings:
health, prosperity, fulfillment
world peace, political sanity.
Tonight, I won't ask for a thing.

Tonight, I'll lie listening to the rain
the rain
the rain.
Tonight, it feels like just being alive
and listening to the rain
is enough.

Marching Music

Each morning I fall into step:
a geriatric procession of
cranky hips, deteriorating discs,
and kneecaps popping in protest.

Some plod along on high alert
for phone-snatchers, bicyclists
root-infested walkways
while others seek tranquility
in the brilliance of poppies
or warm spring wind on our faces.

But dreamers like me are distracted
by music only we can hear:
echoes of verse from our younger days
come to tease us with sweet nostalgia.

I pace my steps to the beat
as Jagger croons his cruel taunt.
Time is on his side, he sneers
but what does a twenty-something know
about the blind-siding treachery of time?

For most of us who once danced
to this optimistic tune in the high school gym
decades have swum by
in cycles of ecstasy and grief:

romances thrived, marriages crumbled
careers soared and sank
the wonders of birth, the heart-shattering
demise of loved ones.

Still, as Mick repeats, repeats
with seductive insistence his lies
I'll cling to Father Time's fingertips
until the hour he shakes me free.

And then, in those final seconds
I'll sing out my thanks
for the priceless gift
of a lifetime.

An Empty Tip Jar

I walk this city unseen these days
my wrinkles a cloak
against young men's advances
old men's leers
and the probing eyes of women who
in my long-ago youth
were programmed by nature
to view me as competition.

So intent was I on attracting one
repelling another
my inward focus blinded me
to subtle frailties
like the aura of sadness
enveloping the singer
offering up tunes on the corner
his guitar case laid open, empty
hungry and anxious, yet hopeful.

Before, I would not have seen it:
his rising shame
as they filed past, oblivious
engrossed in conversation
or electronic diversion
worth more to them than a song
too busy for a moment's pause
to listen, applaud, toss him a buck
not even a smile
to acknowledge the music
he practiced for months
building the courage to be here.

I sway to a tune I once danced to
back in high school
before he was born.
I applaud and whisper: "I see you.
I hear you. Thank you."
I drop a five into his desolate case
and he nods, surprised—
I guess because
until that moment
he hadn't even noticed I was there.

Carnival Days

This tilt-a-whirl planet spins and pivots
rattles my spirit, dizzies my soul.
Those sudden swerves they slip and slide me
How can one expect, at the end of the day
to walk a straight line or think clearly?

My friend rides the carousel, dreamy eyed
as around she goes in predictable circles
ups and downs gentle, the music merry
nostalgic, hypnotic, and chosen to give her
nothing she won't want to hear.

Now come the screams, glee swirled with fear
from the roller coaster, zipping, dipping:

"Wahoo!" shouts one.
"Let me off!" wails another.
As into the Fun House I stumble again
she tightens her grip on the unicorn's mane
and sways to the sweet calliope.

Mis Information

Intoxicating
seductive
Mis Information
sprays sweet perfume
to cover the reek
of malignant contagion
as she stretches
lithesome limbs
across the vast, viral blanket.

A practiced flirt
she beckons
and purrs:

Come and get it, baby.
I know what you want.
Invite all your friends
and let's party.

Familiar Shores

I stroll familiar shores
entranced by the ocean's song:

the baritone barks of seals
cavorting toward the harbor
high-pitched squeals, as children
test the tide with icy toes
ecstatic yips of puppies unleashed
dissonant shrieks of terns and gulls

all merging somehow
in symphonic harmony
with the thrum of the sea
and its waves
of percussive crescendo.

Lost in the music
I stroll familiar shores
and nostalgia rolls in with the fog:

friends and lovers
cousins, sisters
summer nights by driftwood fires
jokes and tokes and reminiscing
woolen blanket, wine-warm kisses
the mournful call of a lighthouse horn
for sailors a warning
but to us
just a part of the song.

I stroll familiar shores.
Memories walk beside me
while up ahead
a poem flirts and teases
and dances just out of my reach.

Oops, You Missed It

Not now, you say.
It's cold and you're spent
as the wolf moon returns
to spill down its magic
on rovers and lovers
and muse-seeking poets.
We shall have, you promise
so many moons more
to soothe our senses
thrill our spirits
with quaint superstitions
and romantic whims.

But now
as the final moon beckons?
Will you deny, at the end
that stooped, withered creature
who springs from your mirror
frantic
demanding her parka and cane?

Though in her soul she suspects
the moon never weeps
for the transient shadows below:
Earth's fragile creations
who dance for a time
then dissolve with their dreams
into nothing.

Still, she would bathe
in its splendor.

Will you walk with her down
to the vineyard tonight
as she offers her tribute
of ecstasy, despair
gratitude and fear
regret for not coming sooner—

all balled up together
and hurled at the sky
in one final
primal howl
at the wolf moon?

Seventy-Eight Degrees and Sunny

Why squander a day such as this
uploading, downsizing, muttering curses,
entangled in fathomless technical terms
when you have no talent for website design
and have used up your last ounce of patience?

Why seclude yourself, as the hours slip away
in the cave of sly self-absorption
contorting your brain in a vanity project
pointless for one with nothing to sell
but an eclectic collection of phrases?

It's a day better spent in a park, at the zoo
on an overdue hike or a bike ride.
Or would you remain in the dungeon
to ponder, with narcissistic focus
the photo you chose for your bio:

eyes unreadable behind stylish shades
yet something in your stance—
hand on the gate latch
tilt of your sunhat—
asks: why languish on this sun-drunk day
growth stunted, spirit wilted
while revival is a single *save (click)*
and a skip
down the front steps away
to where rhymes like wildflowers
scamper through ditches—

one calls your name, flirtatious, seductive.
Will you spring from the web
and give chase, I wonder
or will she go home with another?

Look Up!

This harvest moon
will rock your night.
Fat, yellow, lowdown.
Stunning.
Unbiased, it glows
enchantment, gratis
for the peaceful-hearted
as well as the frantic.
Step outside.
Look up.
This moon can't lie.
It speaks its mind
and its thoughts
are pure brilliance.
Allow yourself
a moment of awe.
Smile at God.
Thank the universe.
Grant nature
an appreciative salute.
Break out in song.
Compose a sonnet.
Paint a prayer.
Take photos to share.
Delight your friends
disarm your enemies
we could all use some
perspective-softening
moondust.

This moon is magic.
Unbiased, it waits
to rock your night.
Step outside.
See the light.
Look up!

About the Author

Peggy Schimmelman is the poet laureate of Livermore, CA. Her work includes the poetry chapbooks *Crazytown* (Writing Knights Press, 2016) and *Tick-Tock* (Finishing Line Press, 2019) and the novels *Insomniacs, Inc.* (Russian Hill Press, 2022) and *Whippoorwills* (Independent, 2015). She is co-author *of Long Stories Short* (Independent, 2017) and *Two Truths and a Lie* (Independent, 2020) by Wild Vine Writers. Her poetry and short fiction have appeared in the *North American Review, Naugatuck River Review, Peregrine, WinningWriters.com*, the *Aleola Journal of Poetry and Art, Haight Ashbury Literary Journal, Pacific Review, Comstock Review,* the *Wild Musette, 100wordstories.org,* and others.

This collection of poems reflects her life-long love of music. She is a percussionist in the volunteer band Heart Strings and has written songs with Livermore singer/songwriter Patrick Russ, including "Make Me Your Love Song," adapted from "A Poem in Three," which was originally published in *Wild Musette Journal.* The song was recorded by the duo Patrick and Leanne, featuring the beautiful vocals of Leanne Phillips. The song can be heard on various digital platforms.

Peggy welcomes feedback and inquiries at her website:
peggyschimmelman.com

www.ingramcontent.com/pod-product-compliance
Lightning Source LLC
Chambersburg PA
CBHW031205160426
43193CB00008B/506